A Helpful Guide

By
Karen Rae Ziegler

RECLAIMING WOOD *WORKS*
A Helpful Guide

Author: Karen Rae Ziegler

ISBN-13: 978-1987487435
ISBN-10: 1987487435

For permission, please contact:
Karen Ziegler
wkziggy@cox.net

Printed as a work of non-fiction in the U.S.A.

Forward

I have had the most pleasurable moments working with wood and preparing it for use on walls and/or in craft projects. The joy it brings, to create and share its life span, is unmeasurable and subjective.

Each timber piece is unique and although one board might not seem "worthy" of being placed on a wall, with its many nature's friends, it has a place somewhere.

Some are so awesome that I won't "waste" it on a wall and it will become a center piece project all on its own. Whether you desire a masterpiece for your own home or family member or you start working in the reclaiming business, I'll walk you through what has worked for me.

Enjoy!

1
The Hunt

Pallets can be found in many store parking lots, trash areas, recycling places and sometimes in your friend's yard! When materials are sold on pallets distributors often charge deposits so that people return them for reuse. We can't just assume the pallet is being discarded. There still seems to be plenty of usable product around. I've also seen offerings online, like Craigslist and Letgo.com, where others collect the pallets and do some initial clean up by taking them apart and removing some protruding nails.

The prices are OK but if you aren't in a hurry just keep your eyes open and start collecting tallying how many square feet you need. It's exhausting working on a couple hundred square feet project when you're under a time restraint so think ahead and start gathering.

It's a labor of love because it can be quite laborious but can also be a meditation as the project comes alive and brings so much joy. You'll see!

A word of caution about buying newer wood at Home Depot, Dixieline or Lowe's-type stores. Newer cut wood still has shrinkage so it would be a bummer to put new wood on a wall only to have it shrink up and leave spaces. You'll see this in wood fences where installers leave a space, thinking it looks uniform, and then as the fence dries out those spaces get bigger and inconsistent. The fence boards are also made of the same timber and that's not normally the look we're going for with a reclaimed wall. I'd also investigate the age of painted barn wood due to the use of lead-based paint many decades ago.

Start making your piles of potentially 2" wide and up to 8" wide boards. Any length is fine and so is any width actually. Even a twisted board can potentially be cut down and used. I try and stay uniform with the thicknesses as it becomes important later during installation. I also pick 3-4 different widths to make it easier. Each row of the wall should be the same width unless you are working on a puzzle look. I steer away from that. I like my rows uniform.

Don't judge the dog! Deciding against a straight board by its raw looks is a mistake! It's impossible to see the beauty, in most of the pieces, at this point. There is much work to do and every board has its place. There will be reasons to toss a few, that's their place, but give this some time to surface and get the collecting going. You'll find thick and thin, sap and painted, dirty and filled with nails, as well as stamps of coding designating the "free of chemicals" codes or country of origin.

These marking/coding methods are easily sanded or cut off so just ignore them on the board, for now, unless it's marked MB which means it's chemically treated. I haven't found one yet but just a heads up that you need to pass on that potentially harmful pallet. Moving on...

The beauty of using pallets is that the wood is of different types and ages. This makes a big difference in the finished product because, in a reclaimed wall, the variation is what makes it come alive with beauty. Different ages and types can look very different even when the same solution is used on each board. How cool is that? The old barns were made of different types of timber too. That's where this idea started from as the old barns created so much variation and eventual beauty from afar. Only when you get up close do you see the decayed condition and wonder what purpose that wood could actually have in the future. Well? If the barn is being torn down you might have an eventual gold mine worth of beautiful wood pieces.

So, as I stated, avoid chemically-treated pallets when possible. These are normally marked with an MB for Methyl Bromide. There are IPPC logos (International Plant Protection Convention) on some pallets but just because they aren't there doesn't mean it isn't safe. When countries belong to this agency they agree to the need to treat wood materials of a thickness greater than 6mm and the coding is used to ship products between countries. The country list is growing as shipping worldwide becomes more commonplace.

To feel extra safe look for codes like HT, for heat treated, used to kill most bugs and pathogens, DB for debarked (not used much anymore) and KD for kiln dried, dried to 19% or less, which reduces the chances of mold. These are supposedly safe treatment methods. There are also color codes for the country of origin so check the internet for that info as it might change. Even though many countries are joining the global fight against chemically treated pallets, and they are registering their compliance, you never know what chemical has spilled onto the pallet in transport or prior use.

Use caution and when in doubt just toss it aside. It's also important to know that the markings won't be on all the boards. Only one board will show it and then it's often broke off, or the pallet isn't whole, so know that most pallets found today are reportedly safe.

If the board is badly split just discard it unless you have some other art project it might work for.

Here is an example of a board that wouldn't work on a typical reclaimed wall, because it was too thin in areas. This is also an example of a board I didn't want to "waste" on a reclaimed wall, but it made a nice sign full of character with the old termite channels and multiple knots. This piece was so hard I had trouble putting the nails in to hold the string. I was pretty sure a bug wasn't still in it! No stain or sanding was needed. Nice!

2
Rough Prep

Rough preparation entails dismantling of the pallets and examining each piece so that you aren't addressing issues later. Dismantling isn't pulling the nails out to separate the boards. They are usually in there very tight. You'll need to use a reciprocator saw or a hand metal saw to get between the boards and saw them apart.

Protruding nails and staples must be removed or it will damage your sandpaper and potentially your hand sander disk as well. The use of a nail punch and hammer works great. The beauty of the staples and nail heads is usually desired so the surface metal should remain. If they pop out slightly then place the board on a steel surface and pound the nail from the opposite side. This should suffice. Don't worry about leaving a hole where a nail is removed. You will have plenty of nice nail heads to add character to your wall and empty nail holes will blend just fine.

Boards with cracks are ok also. When installing the wall, you will be cutting off the ends of many to make them fit. These cracked ends will often times be eliminated at this time. If the board is badly cracked just cut it off now. A crack can add character on the finished wall unless it causes an increase in width on that area of the board. This is the time for preparing the boards to save hassle later.

Also, you'll find that some boards are 1" thick. I usually find that these thicker boards are 5", or so, wide too. This can be a problem as you'll be able to see the edges of the board sticking out, past the next row, on the wall unless the entire wall is made with 5" wide boards. Either pull it, to be used elsewhere, or plan to work around the thickness which we'll discuss later in installation. I plan other projects around these thicker pieces and try to use the lighter weighted boards on the walls.

Another issue is clusters of nails found in some boards. If the project of removing those nails is too great either toss the board, cut off the cluster or save it for a challenging day of nail removal. Nail clusters can greatly affect your safety when using the table saw, to rip the board for even width, so deal with it now.

3
Finish Prep

I use a table saw to rip the boards into the desired thickness. This keeps the rows uniform so that the edges aren't so obvious. I normally only need to rip one side but curves cause issues later so this is the time to get that consistency in width. Please use caution as this machine is very dangerous but it's the best way to get uniformity. If you don't have one you'll need to sort your rows carefully. This doesn't have to be perfect but within 1/8-inch is probably as imperfect as I would like. I love texture but trying to install a wall like a puzzle will likely look disturbing, take time and be frustrating. I like consistent rows of 3"-7" widths but make the whole row the same.

If it's a thick board, and you love it so much that you must use it, you'll either need to finish the sides too or plan to use shims to bring out a thinner board against a thicker one. This is fine but stay away from using too thick of a board, like 1", unless you want it all that thick. You'll thank me later. If you end up using them just be careful where you do it. Maybe in a corner when your hanging the wood vertical or in the creation of Wainscoting or around the bottom of a bar. If you must a shim then extra installation time will be in order.

I separate the boards so that I'm not changing my saw width often...attacking the 3" width and then the 4", etc. I also use the next board to push the prior board through so that I'm far away from that nasty blade! This is also the time to cut the dog-ears off the boards if there are any. Again, if a board is just plain too crazy it can be used for another project or tossed. Also, be aware that if you have missed a nail, and that saw blade hits it, that board could go flying or kick back and it could also damage your blade. Prep is very important but safety trumps it.

4
Sand

A quick glance at the two board sides will help you decide which side to enhance. It's fun to compare the two sides, at completion, as the contrast is ridiculously amazing in many cases. You'll swear it's not the same board!

These two examples are the back of the raw board vs. front. Just take your pick. They looked close but I chose the smoothest...less sanding!

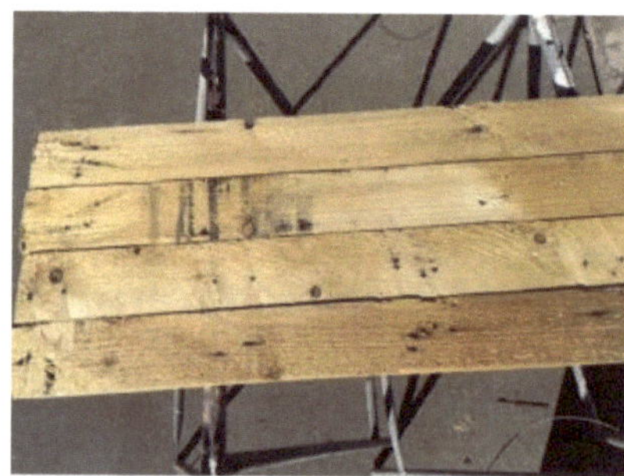

I use an electric hand sander that starts when I apply pressure to the wood. I'm not super picky about the grit harshness but on the first sanding some boards may need around a 50-60 grit paper. The disk that holds the paper can get damaged from protruding nails and when applying pressure on the board edges so plan on ordering replacements when needed. I find Amazon a good source.

Make sure you don't just look at the brand of sanding disk as there are 3 screw holes or 4 screw holes, to attach to the sander, depending on the unit. I like to keep the spares on hand. When you're in the mood to sand you want to keep moving! It can be exhausting!

Now, for those thicker boards...I like to bevel the edges and treat them too. This is to avoid seeing the edge of the board when it's on the wall. All the other boards are not beveled as it's hard on my sander and me. The square edges work just fine.

5
Clean

I use a hand brush to dust off wood and sponge apply Mineral Spirits or paint thinner as a nice cleaning agent that dissolves any leftover waxes, oils or polishes. This prepares it for our next coloring treatment.

The paint thinner/Mineral Spirits is optional but I'm a bit excessive compulsive. You'll see the grains in the wood start to come alive with this dusting and cleaning. The solution dries quickly and we're just looking for a clean surface. These boards are going to be hanging in a house!

6
To Treat ... or Not to Treat

It's rare for me to omit putting some agent on the wood but it does happen. The signage piece, shown previously, has no substance applied and I even omitted the sanding. It was simply cleaned and decorated with nails and string.

My base is apple cider vinegar and steel wool. I've tried old rusty nails, old pennies, screws, wire, but steel wool is simple and it starts turning the liquid pretty fast. As it sits it darkens. You can dilute it from there. I use this solution to create more variety adding mustard to one jar, red paint to another and blue to another

It only takes about a teaspoon of color, in a large mason jar of vinegar, to create enough color. Remember, the variety of the timber types will change the color from the same jar. It doesn't take much color and most of my boards are straight apple cider vinegar with steel wool. The different timbers are what absorbs each solution differently.

I'll sometimes pick up a piece and decide to use different solutions on the same board. Perhaps the knots are treated separately than the rest of the board. It's easy to get creative and very hard to mess up completely. Perhaps a wave of red streaking across the board, and then a finish of straight apple cider vinegar/steel wool over the whole board. A cheap paint brush works great.

After I'm done I let them sit in the sun or overnight. There isn't much excitement, at this point, as the beauty is hidden under the coating, but it's doing its magic on the tannins in the wood.

A funny story was when I was asked to create a white wall and I decided to apply peroxide over my already colored boards. I came out, the next morning, and all the boards were solid white! I had to sand them down and regroup! All worked out fine, with the addition of some straight white paint, but I've learned to keep it simple.

7
Final Sanding

This is one of my favorite steps as the patina of the wood starts to come alive. I use a 100-120 grit sand paper and lightly go over the surface of the board spending a bit more time on the knots to bring them alive. Don't sand too much but use your judgement on each board.

If you can't feel the love from a particular board then hit it again with either more color or some rough sanding. I rarely find a board I don't want to use. There is enough beauty at completion that a subtle board, here and there, helps give it some soft harmony.

8
Brush to Clean

Only brush at this point. The Mineral Spirits or a thinner could change the color. I found this out when I added a beautiful blue hue to a project and when I applied my final cleaning of paint thinner it completely eliminated the blue.

Ugh! I had to reapply color and learned an important lesson ... just brush it clean.

9
Sealing or Oiled

This is another favorite step. Nothing brings out the grains like sealing. I've used up all the leftovers in my house for sealing! Old lotions, oils (skin-so-soft & linseed), gels, ointments etc. Okay, I know I'm weird but I can't throw anything out!

Now I'm down to what works so perfectly that I'll continue its use, coconut oil. Since coconut oil turns solid at under 78 degrees I either apply it with a brush or sponge depending on the weather.

A microwave comes in handy too. I rub it in and the wood colors and grains come alive like you won't believe! This is an exciting step of reveal! I could do it all day … every day!

Newly applied vinegar solution vs. 2 hrs. post application.

These are the finish sanded unsealed vs. the sealed with oil.

And finally, a comparison of the Raw vs. Oiled end product. It will create a nice blend on the wall.

10
Prepping the Wall

A good start is to paint the wall black or at least dark. It can be a bad paint job so don't worry. This is to avoid seeing the wall between the boards, if they aren't perfectly ripped, or seeing the wall through a knot in the wood.

I've seen others put up vertical 1x3 boards, in strips, on the existing drywall, and the reclaimed wall attached to it, but I don't usually bother. I use a stud finder and mark the wall but the boards don't necessarily need to be attached to a stud. It's nice to know where the studs are in case a heavy picture is hung later and a stud finder won't work through the thickness of the reclaimed wood. So, beginning the hanging process, by putting nails in the studs, will be a clue for later hanging.

Of course, I dare anyone to hang something on my reclaimed wood project! Please wait until I'm gone!

11
Install

I plan my installation around my inventory. Each row should be a single width. If I have more of one width then plan your project around that by installing more rows of that board thickness.

A nail gun and air-compressor works great for this installation. If you don't have one I'd rent or borrow one. I use 1.5" nails as it's enough to hold the board in the drywall without going too deep as to interfere with electrical or plumbing. It won't work well to use a nail and hammer or screws. Using screws will require predrilling so that you don't split these old boards. It will be much more time consuming too!

I like to start at the ceiling so if I need to rip the boards, at the wall base, it won't be so obvious. Also, stand back and avoid placing like-boards together or close color matches next to each other. The other important suggestion is to keep the seams staggered. I try and plan for the alternate row of seams to be at least 6" from each other.

Now for those 1" boards that you couldn't avoid? Use wedges of cardboard or just position away from the wall as you nail in any row against a 1" thick board. This is to hide seeing the edge of that board which is unfinished. If the 1" thick piece is high up on the wall, nobody will see the top edge, but if it's low, then the board below will need wedged out. We can conceal the edging later but it's nice to work it now if possible. Try turning a thick board over as I find some edges are easily camouflaged with this technique. 1.5" nails should be just enough.

Don't forget to offset the board ends from row to row.

The corners are of special consideration. There are trim pieces available to complete the edge or you can 45 degree the end of the board to make a corner as seen in the picture below on the right. In the picture to the left the inside corner pieces just butted up against each other however, I did "wrap" many of the boards through the corner using the same board to cut and continue through the corner. This keeps your eye from getting stuck there.

12
Review

Now is the time to step back and walk around looking for little things that pop out at you.

Perhaps an extra nail or screw is needed? Felt pens can be used to color a rough edge that is catching your eye. Some holes might be obvious and reveal the wall in the back. I've seen marbles, rocks or flowers placed in these openings but some clients just love the look of a knot hole!

Enjoy

I'm often emotional when I finish a project. Maybe it's the time I've spent on each piece but when it's all put together it's a masterpiece that is unique and impossible to duplicate.

The playful wall, on the left above, has variations in thickness, length and application products. I used some paint but I needed the color and even-though I've implemented some mustard, turmeric, wine, balsamic vinegar, peroxide and whatever else I could find, I still needed some paint to get the contrast they were looking for.

My row width was 3", 4", 5" then repeat...all the way down.

I used natural colors and sealing products on this more formal wall below. A few of the boards had obvious hints of artificial color, already on the boards, but I still stayed as eco-friendly as I could control. Every fourth board was cedar at 7" wide which calmed the wall and really brought a more formal feel to the room.

The owner opted to keep the white baseboard, which matched the rest of the room, where I usually take the wall to the floor, but it looked fantastic at completion. She also plans to take the wood with her, if she ever moves, so the baseboard will still be intact.
My pattern board thickness per row was 7", 3", 5", 3", 7", 3", 4", 3", 7", 3", 5", 3", etc. I had an abundance of 3"-ers!

Instead of incorporating a headboard on the bedframe these clients wanted the corner of the room reclaimed. It worked out fabulously!

Thank You!

Thank you for letting me share one of my favorite current pastimes. I find it physically and emotionally challenging and yet rewarding on many levels. Reclaiming allows me to get creative and enter a meditational time as I create and deliver a beautiful piece of artwork with uniqueness in every timber. Enjoy!